This book belongs to

_____

_____

and I am finding out
about Jesus

© Angus Hudson Ltd and Three's Company, 1988

First published by
Scripture Union
130 City Road
London EC1V 2NJ

Fifth printing, 1995

ISBN 0 86201 577 4

Produced by
Three's Company,
12 Flitcroft St, London WC2

World co-edition organized
and produced by
Angus Hudson Ltd

Printed in Italy

Would you like to know
Jesus?

by Graham Jefferson and Eira Reeves
Illustrated by Eira Reeves

Scripture Union

God made lots of people.

God loves you and wants to be your best friend.

God sent his son Jesus to show us how to be friends with him.

God wants his friends to be kind and loving and obedient.

But often we are unkind, unloving and disobedient. That stops us being friends with God.

Jesus took the punishment for the wrong things we have done. He died on the cross for us.

After Jesus died he came alive again.
Then he went back to heaven
to be with his Father God.

Jesus is still alive! In a wonderful way he can be with us now — whatever we're doing.

Would you like to know Jesus?

This is what you need to do ...

First talk to Jesus as you would talk to a friend.
This is called praying.

Say sorry to him for all the wrong things you have done.

Sometimes we need to say sorry to other friends too.

Thank Jesus for loving you. Ask him to come and be your friend for always ...

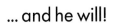

... and he will!

Here is a prayer.

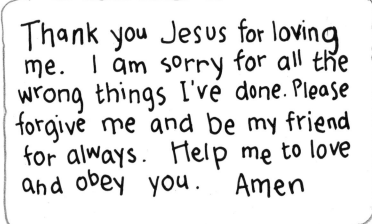

Thank you Jesus for loving me. I am sorry for all the wrong things I've done. Please forgive me and be my friend for always. Help me to love and obey you. Amen

Every day talk to Jesus. Tell him when you're happy and when you're sad.
Find out more about your friend Jesus in the Bible.

Ask your family if you can
go to Sunday School.
You may be at one already —
that's good.

Now have a really happy day with your new friend Jesus.

... and with all his other friends.

Now that you have asked Jesus to be your friend, there's lots to find out about him.

Scripture Union have some books to help you.

You can buy these at your local Christian bookshop.